Turn-to-Learn

Alphabet Wheels

26 Ready-to-Go Reproducible Patterns
That Put a New Spin on Learning the ABCs

Created by Virginia Dooley
Illustrated by Rusty Fletcher

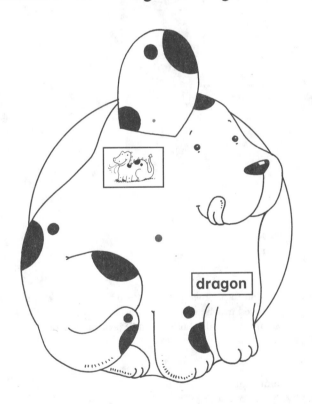

dragon

SCHOLASTIC
PROFESSIONAL **B**OOKS

New York @ Toronto @ London @ Auckland @ Sydney
Mexico City @ New Delhi @ Hong Kong

Thanks to Ingrid Blinken, Jaime Lucero, Rusty Fletcher,
Liza Charlesworth, Terry Cooper, and Sam Martino
for all their help.

Cover design by Vincent Ceci and Jaime Lucero
Cover and interior illustrations by Rusty Fletcher
Interior design by Jaime Lucero for Grafica Inc.
Cover photographs by Donnelly Marks

ISBN 0-590-37904-6

Printed in the U.S.A.

Table of Contents

Welcome to Turn-to-Learn Alphabet Wheels!

Alphabet Wheels are an exciting, hands-on way to teach or reinforce letter sounds and configurations while helping children become acquainted with words that begin with the target letter. The wheels are a powerful learning tool because children love their playful, guessing-game format. The wheels are self-correcting, so they provide instant feedback. And, if a child does miss a word, a turn of the wheel provides a fresh opportunity to try again.

Alphabet Wheels are an ideal addition to a balanced language arts program. They are perfect for use with the whole class, in small groups, and for one-on-one practice. They can be used as the focus of a teacher-directed activity, or placed in a learning center for children to use independently or in pairs. And best of all, Alphabet Wheels are easy to make and simple to store.

Putting the Wheels Together

Whenever possible, involve children in making the wheels themselves.

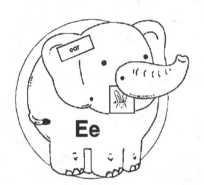

1. To make the wheels you'll need:

- paper or oaktag
- markers or crayons
- scissors
- paper fasteners
- glue

You can make the wheels in the following ways:

✔ Simply photocopy the patterns, cut, and color.
✔ Photocopy the patterns and paste them to oaktag (or recycled manila folders), cut, and color.
✔ Photocopy the patterns onto colored paper, paste them to oaktag, and cut them out.
✔ Photocopy the patterns directly onto oaktag if your copier allows and cut them out.

Cutting Tip!

Some of the cut lines extend to the edge of the wheel to make cutting easier for children. When the lines do not extend to the edge, you or a parent volunteer may need to cut the windows out. The best way to do this is to loosely curve or bend the paper in half at a right angle to the line to be cut. Then "snip" along the line to get the cut started. Re-open and flatten the paper. Insert the tip of the scissors into the slit and cut out the window.

2. Cut out the windows along the dotted lines, and fold along the solid lines.

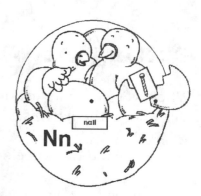

3. Align the wheels and attach the bottom wheel to the top shape by inserting a paper fastener through the $+$ at the center. If a wheel has a moveable answer-hider, attach it by inserting a paper fastener through the ● .

4. Be sure to demonstrate how to use the wheels once they are constructed. Show students how to turn the wheel so the words on the bottom wheel appear in the window.
The wheels work best if the bottom wheel is turned while the top wheel is held in place. Encourage students to read the word before they lift the flap or move the answer-hider to check their answer.

Wheel Variations

Color Contrasts
You can copy the bottom wheel onto a paper color that contrasts with the color you choose for the top shape. This contrast makes it easier for children to focus on the information that appears in the shape's windows.

Laminated Wheels
If you would like to make sturdier wheels, try laminating them or pasting the patterns onto cardboard before assembling.

Textured Wheels
You may want to add texture to some of the wheels by decorating them with colored felt or yarn, cotton balls, or glitter. Children may also want to add texture to the target letters themselves by tracing them with glue and then sprinkling on glitter or sand that they can run their fingers over for some more tactile learning.

Other Ideas for Alphabet Wheels

Oversized Wheels

While students will love having their own Alphabet Wheels, you might want to make an enlarged version to display in a learning center or to use while working with the whole class. To make these oversized versions, simply enlarge the patterns on a copy machine and follow the assembly steps described on pages 5-6.

Customized Wheels

You can customize your Alphabet Wheels by masking over a word and corresponding drawing on the bottom wheel, and writing and drawing in your own word and illustration. Children will especially enjoy seeing their names included on the appropriate letter wheel, along with a drawing or photograph of themselves.

You and your students can use the blank bottom wheel template on page 62 to create a completely customized letter wheel. Students can suggest words that begin with each letter, and draw or find pictures to illustrate the word.

You can also use blank wheels to focus on ending sounds. Have students suggest words that end in each sound, and find or draw corresponding pictures.

Alphabet Wheel Big Books

Invite students to create Alphabet Wheel big books that they can enjoy again and again. Provide each student with big book-sized paper and have students attach their wheels to the pages using a paper fastener so that the wheel can spin. Then, have students fill the surrounding area with names and illustrations of other objects they've found beginning with that letter. If you'd like, you can stack the pages back to back and then staple them together so that the backs of the paper fasteners do not show.

Exploring Letters With Children

While Alphabet Wheels provide an excellent introduction to letter configuration, you may want to give students some additional opportunities to explore letter shapes either before introducing the wheels or after. Here are some suggestions:

✔ Students might enjoy making letters out of clay, pipe cleaners, or aluminum foil.

✔ Give each student a small tray of rice or sand and have them use their fingers to write letters in these mediums.

✔ Keep an eye out for objects that are shaped liked letters. A handle on a mug might look like a C, a clock face might look like an O. Point these objects out to children and invite them to identify others that resemble letters in your classroom and at home.

✔ Help to familiarize children with the various ways letters appear in texts compared with the way they write them. Students can form letter collections by filling a sheet of paper with examples of a specific letter cut from magazines, newspapers, and junk mail.

Literature Links

Here are just a few of the great alphabet books you may want to have available for your students as they begin to learn the alphabet.

Antler, Bear, Canoe by Betsy Brown (Little Brown & Co., 1991)

Demi's Find the Animal ABC by Demi (Grosset & Dunlap, 1985)

Eating the Alphabet by Lois Ehlert (Harcourt Brace Jovanovich, 1993)

Chicka Chicka Boom Boom by B. Martin, Jr., and J. Archambault (Simon & Schuster, 1989)

Farm Alphabet Book by Jane Miller (Scholastic Inc., 1981)

The Graphic Alphabet by D. Pelletier (Orchard, 1996)

The Alphabet Wheels

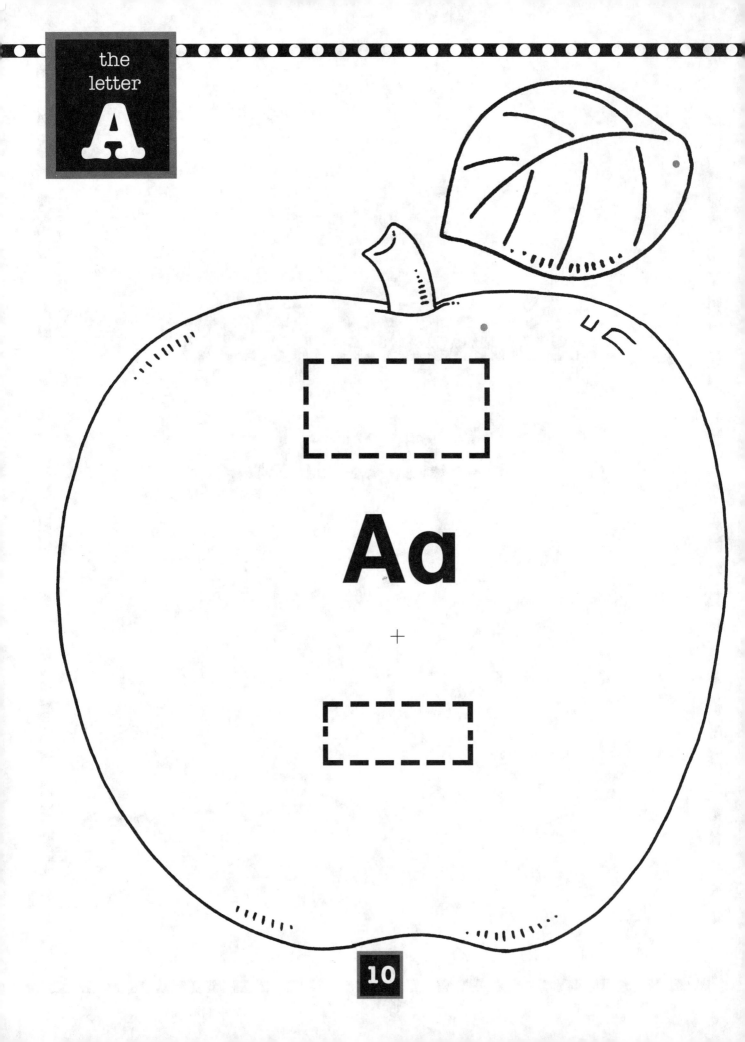

Aa

+

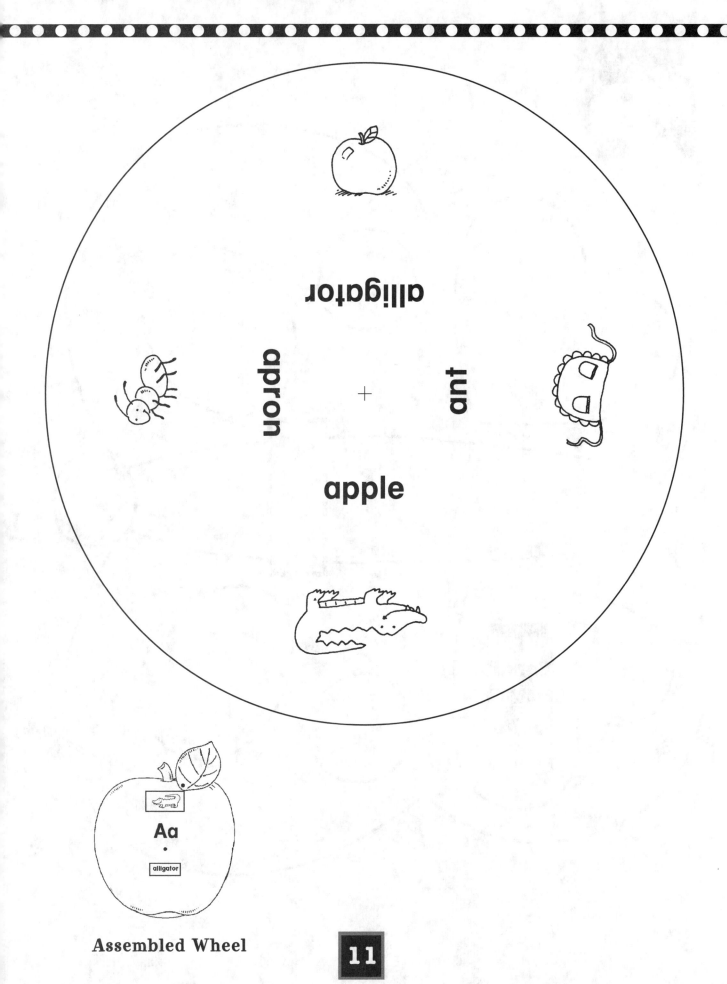

apron

ant

alligator

apple

Aa

alligator

Assembled Wheel

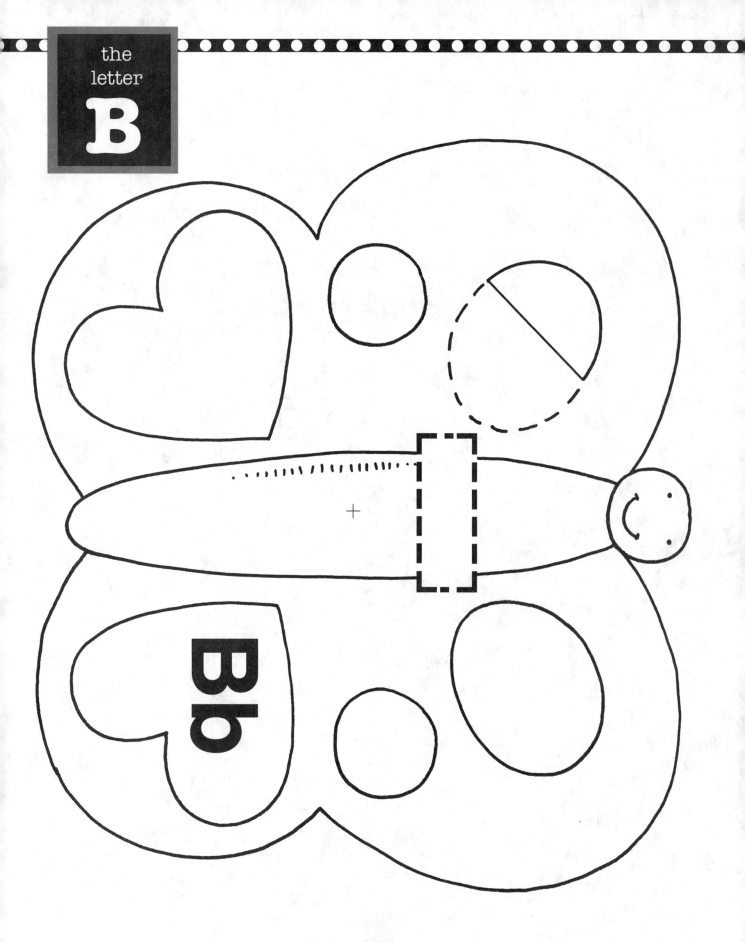

Bb

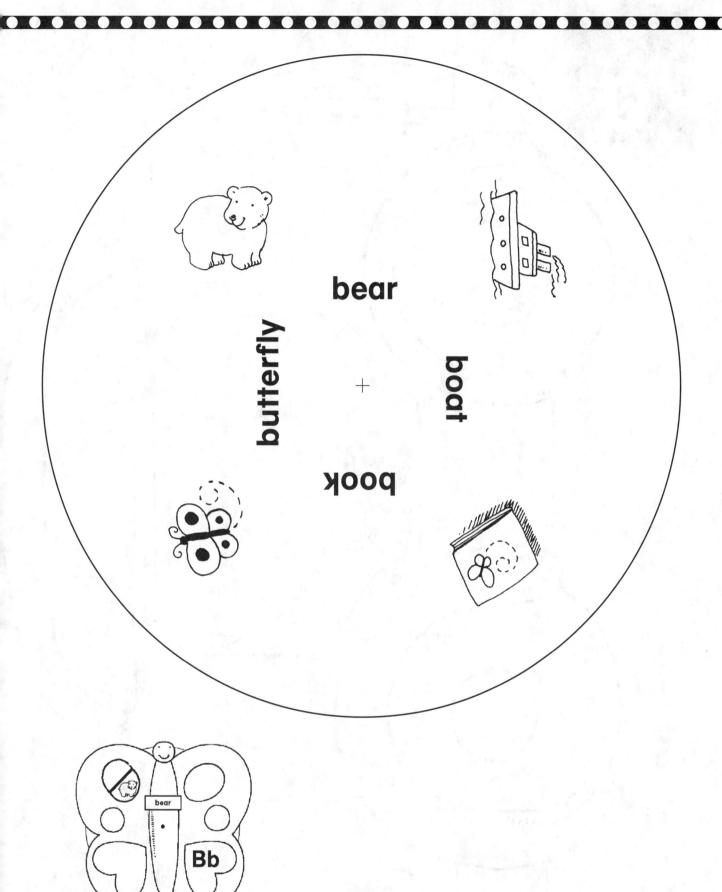

bear

butterfly

boat

book

Assembled Wheel

13

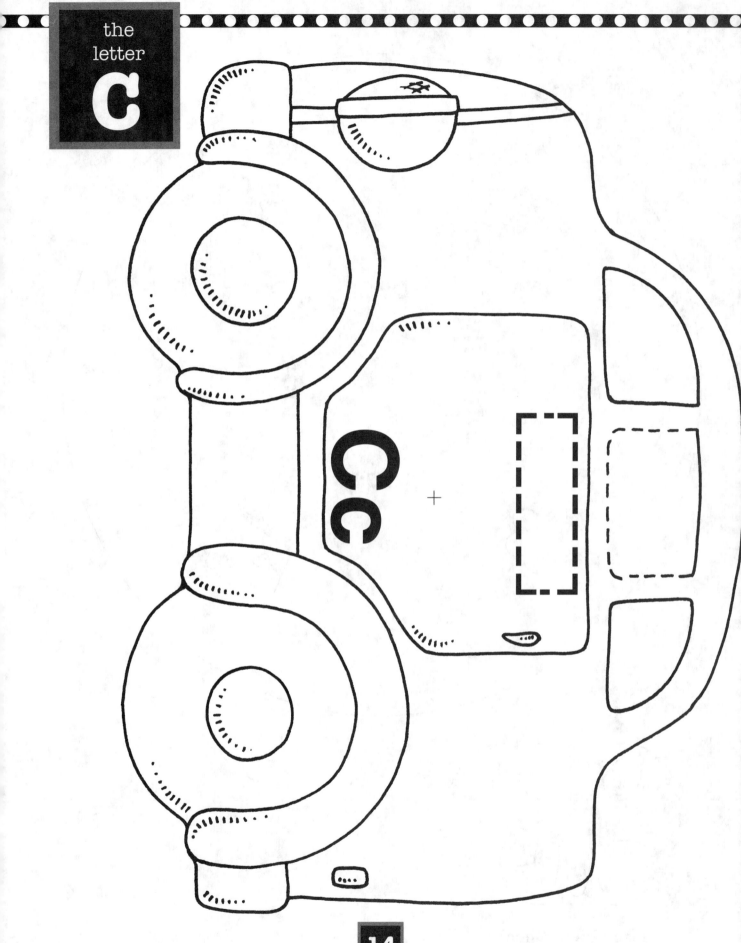

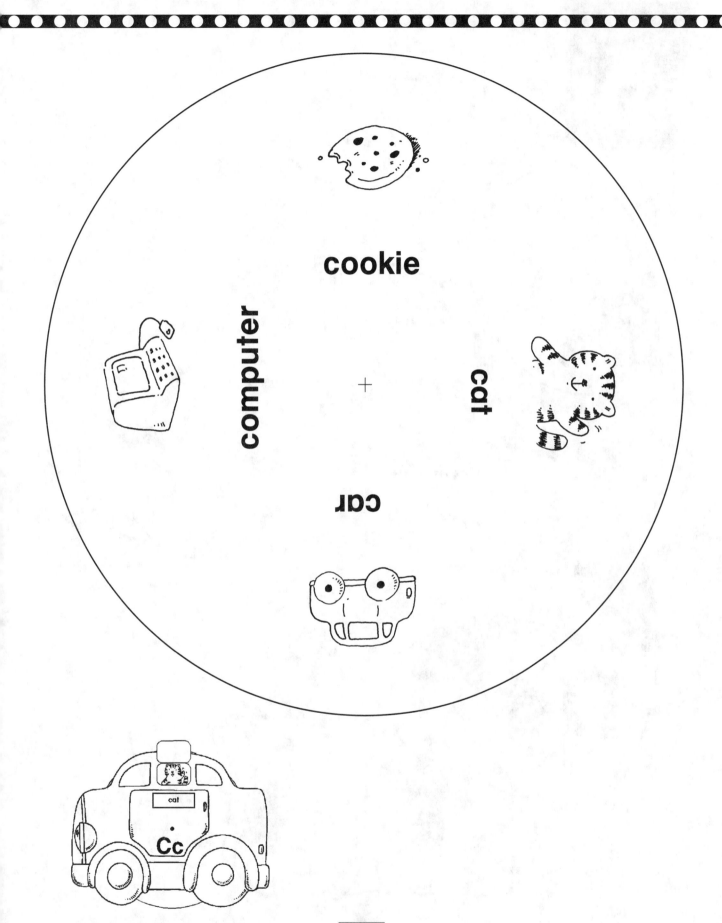

cookie

computer

cat

car

Assembled Wheel

15

Dd

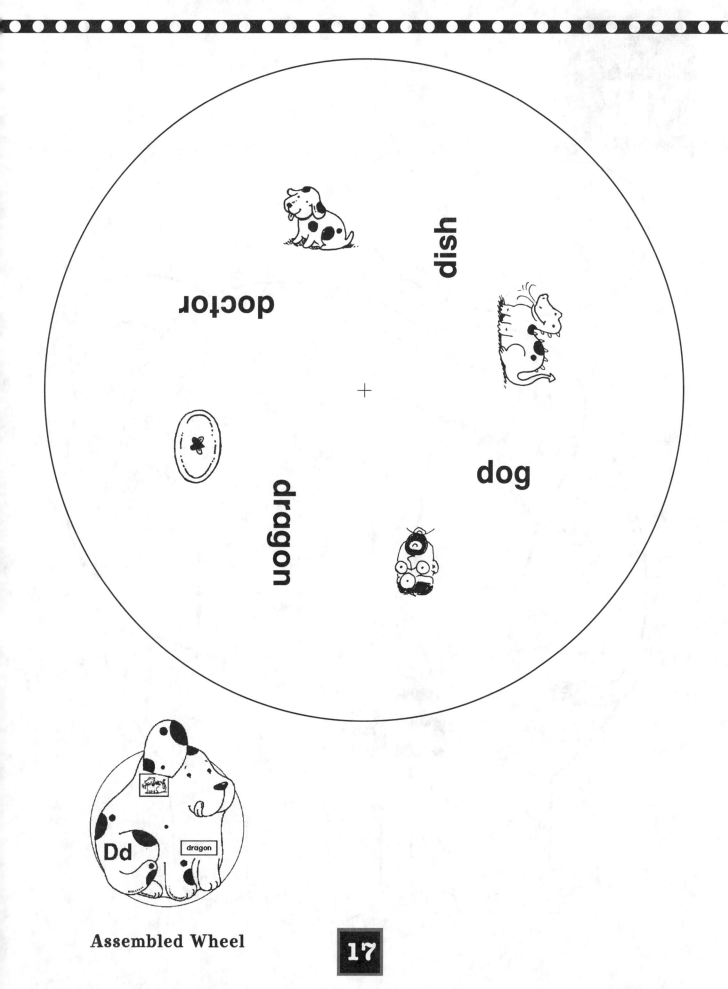

dish

doctor

dog

dragon

Assembled Wheel

17

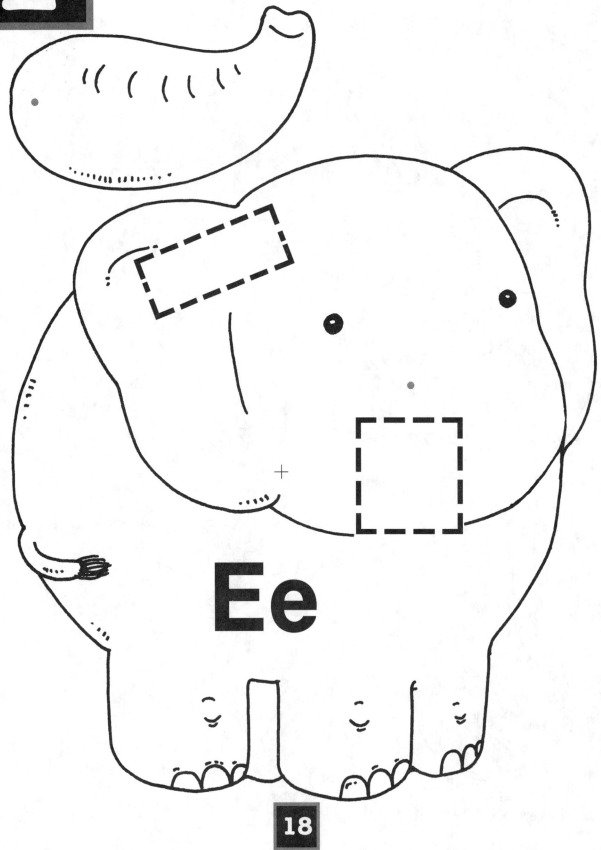

Ee

18

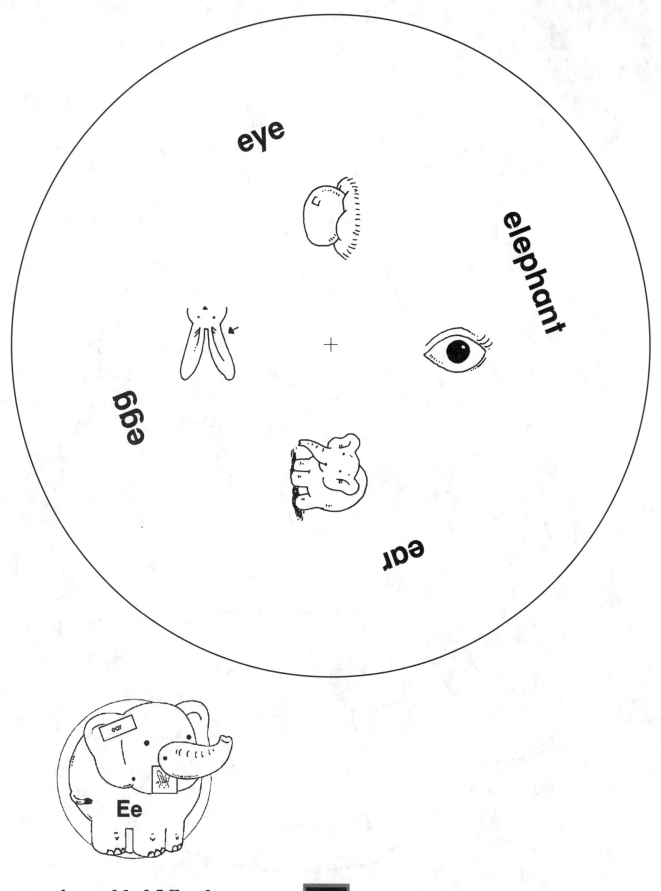

eye

elephant

egg

ear

Assembled Wheel

Ff

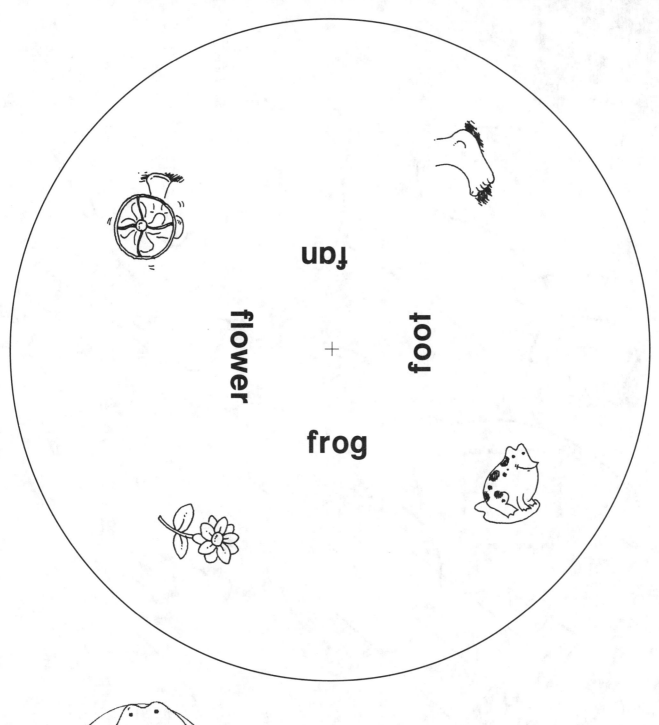

fan

flower + foot

frog

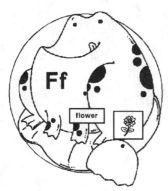

Assembled Wheel

21

Gg

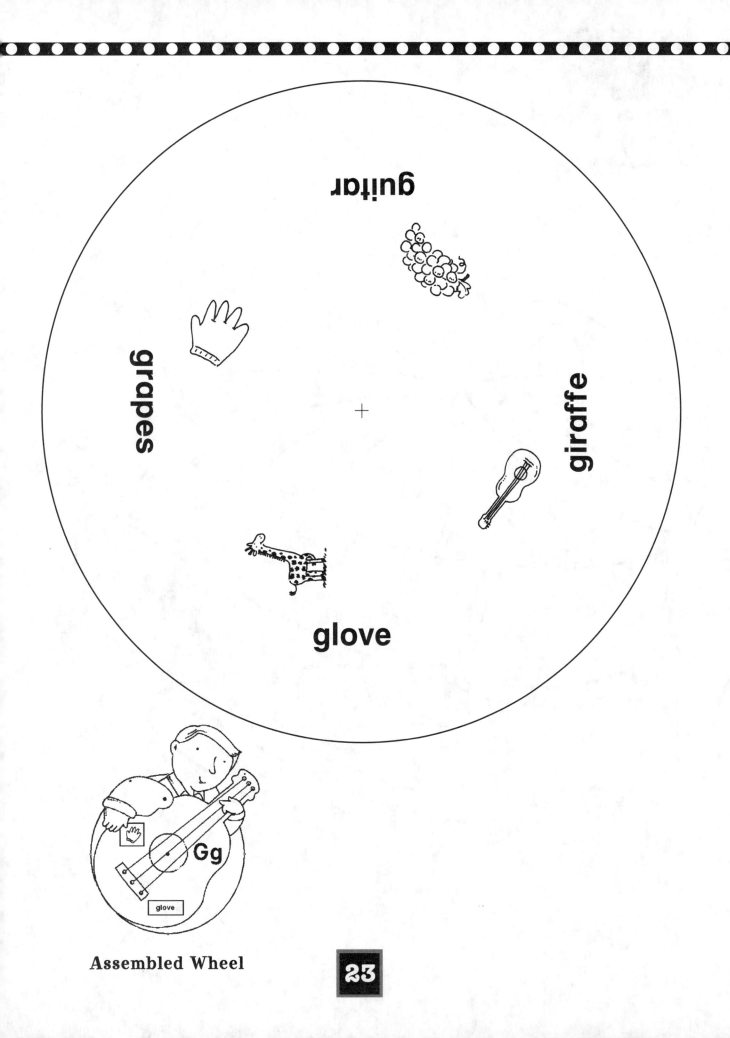

guitar

grapes

giraffe

glove

Gg

glove

Assembled Wheel

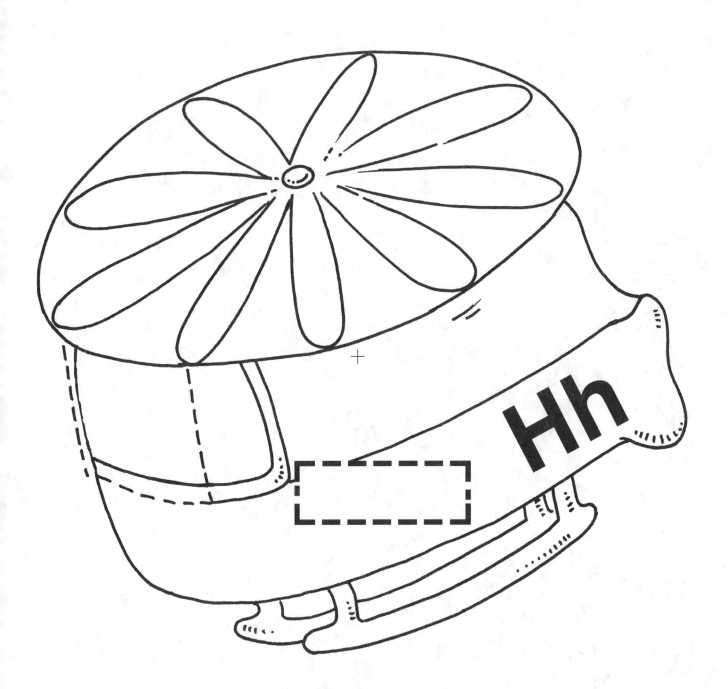

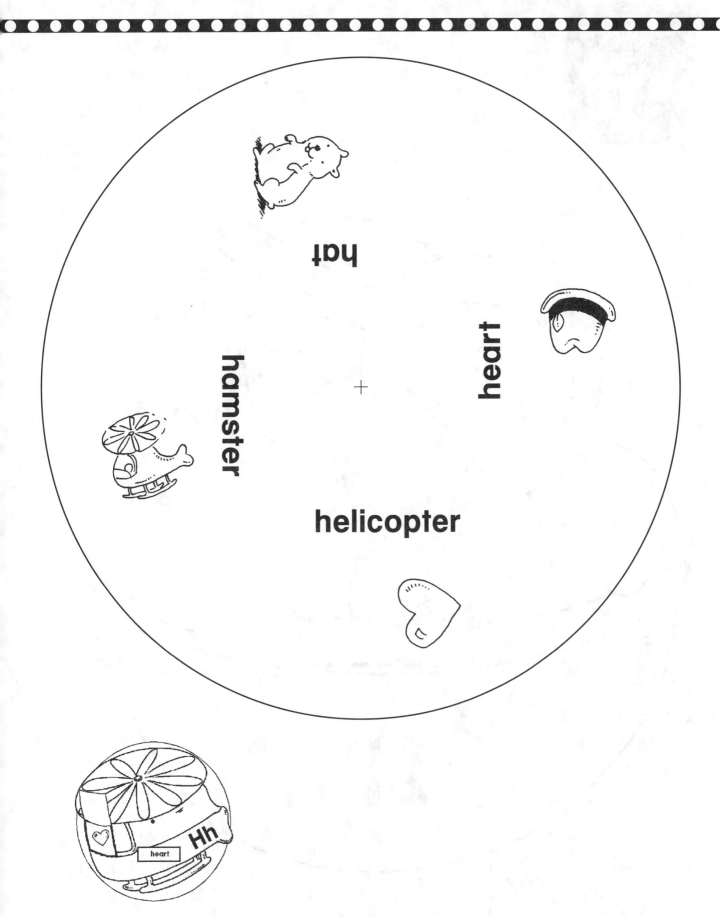

hat

hamster

heart

helicopter

Assembled Wheel

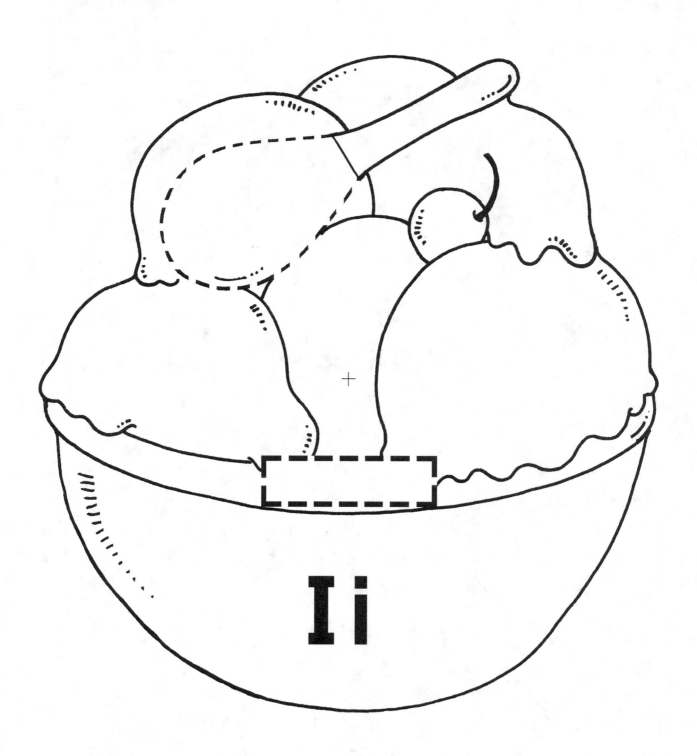

I i

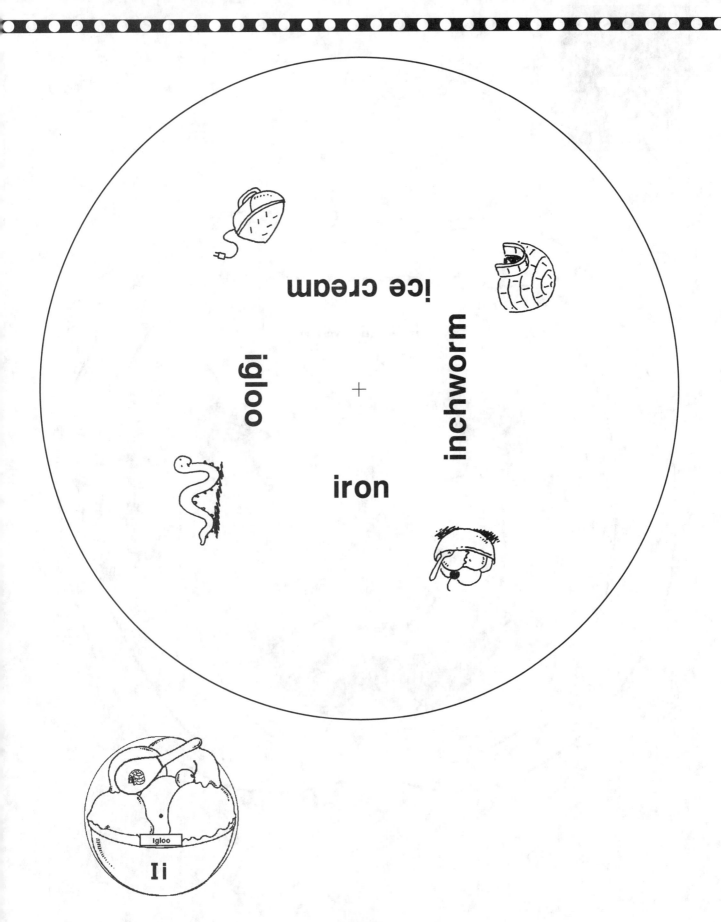

igloo

ice cream

inchworm

iron

Ii

igloo

Assembled Wheel

27

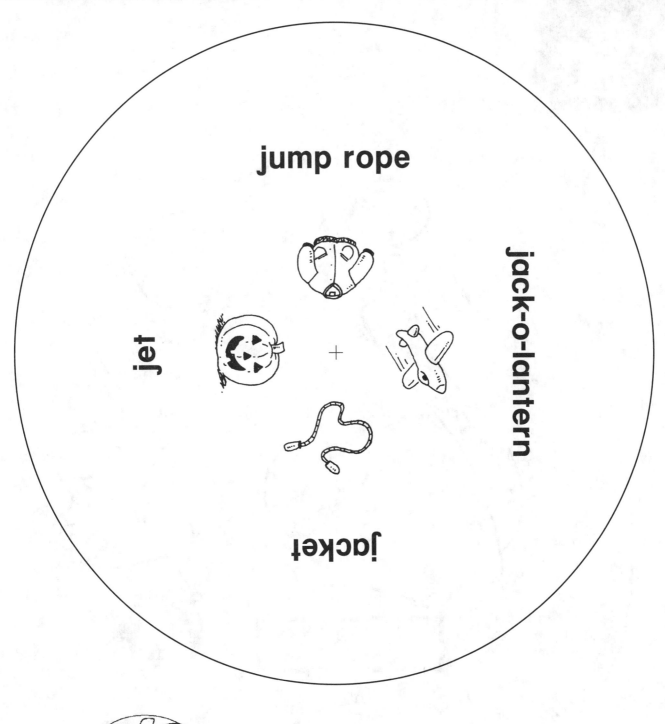

jump rope

jack-o-lantern

jet

+

jacket

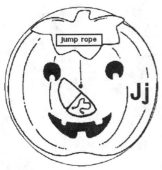

jump rope

Jj

Assembled Wheel

29

Kk

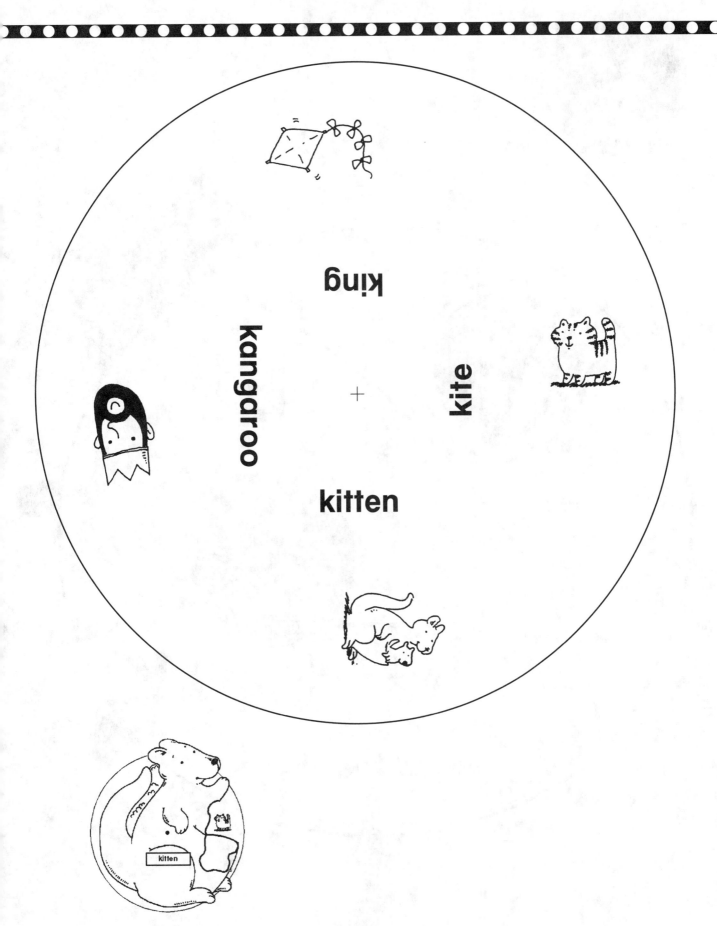

king

kangaroo

kite

kitten

Assembled Wheel

31

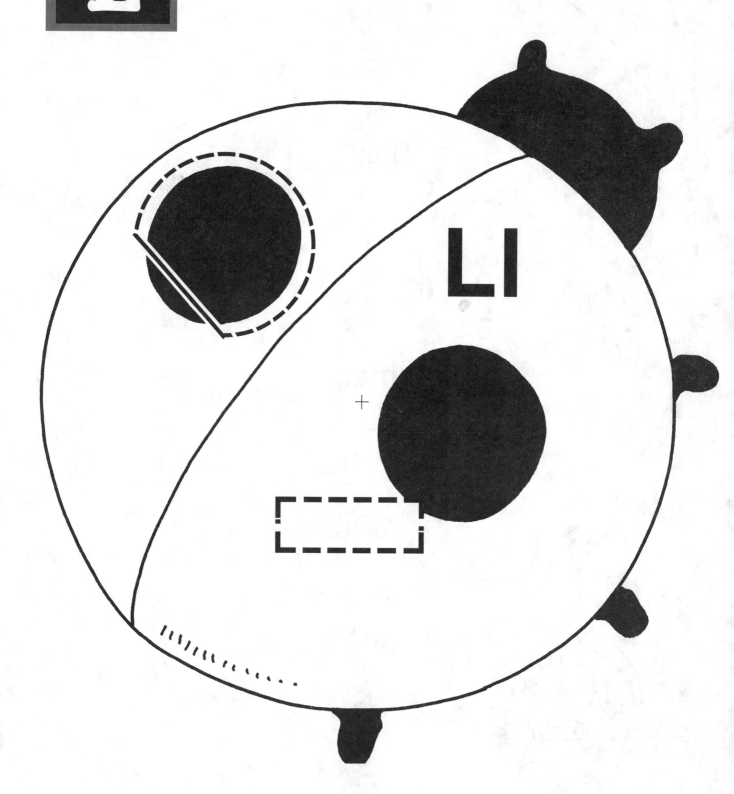

Ll

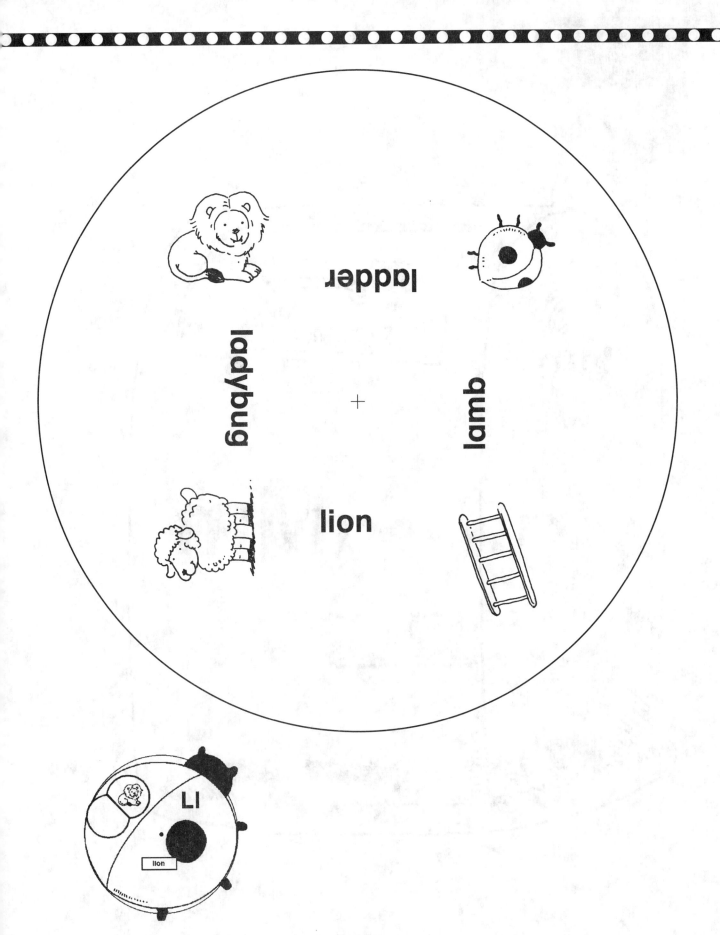

ladder

ladybug

+

lamb

lion

LI

lion

Assembled Wheel

33

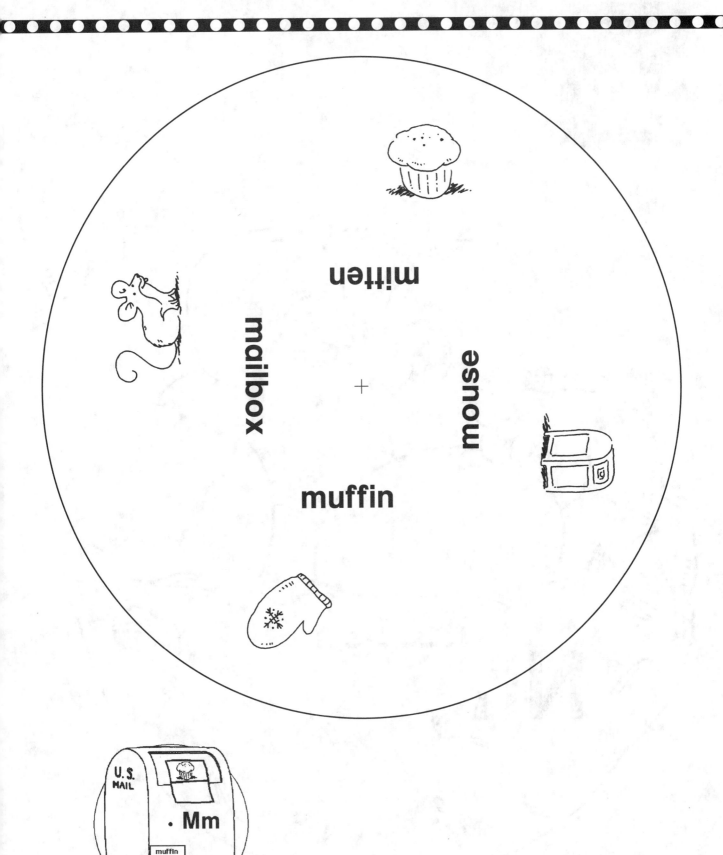

mitten

mailbox

mouse

muffin

Assembled Wheel

Nn

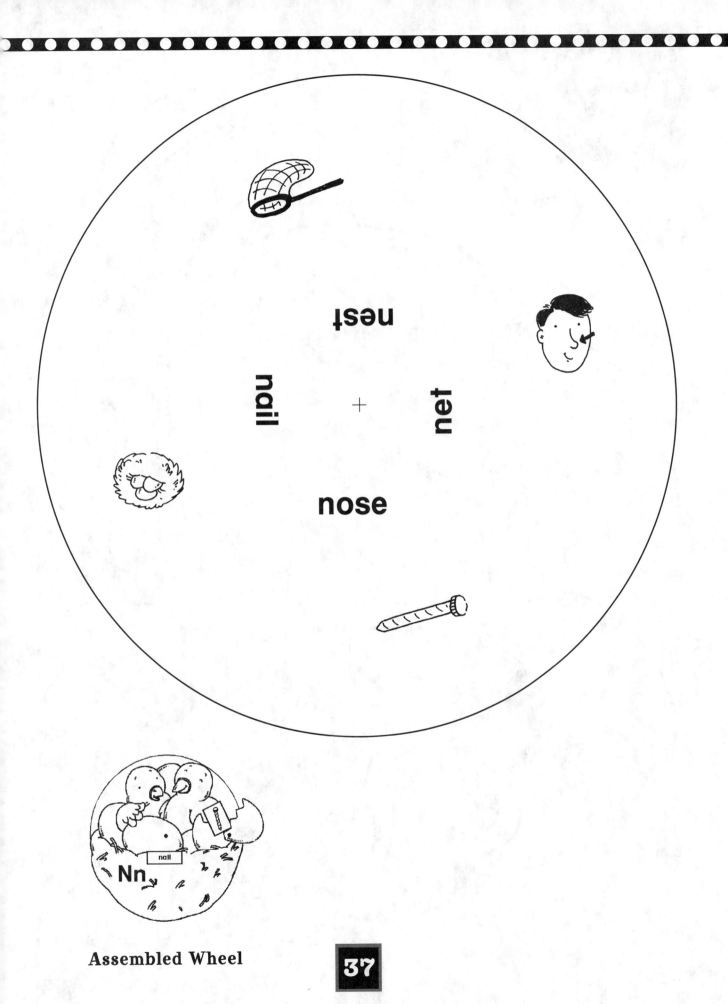

nest

nail + net

nose

Assembled Wheel

the
letter
O

Oo

38

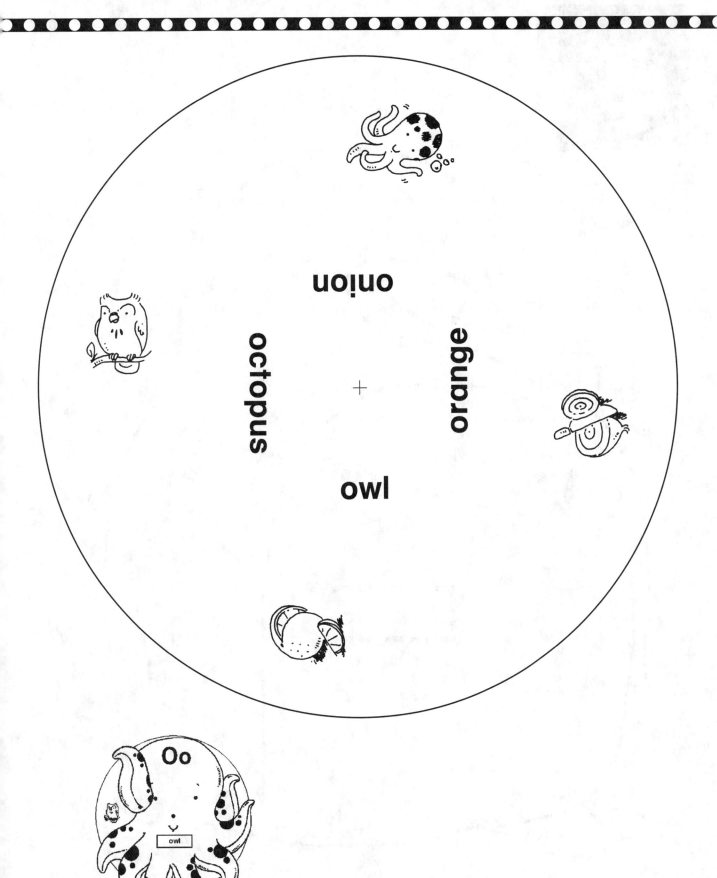

onion

octopus

$+$

orange

owl

Oo

owl

Assembled Wheel

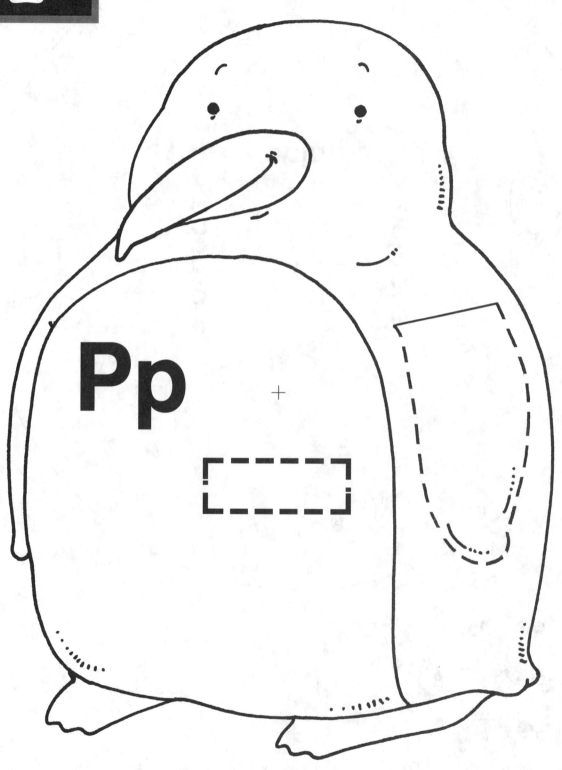

Pp

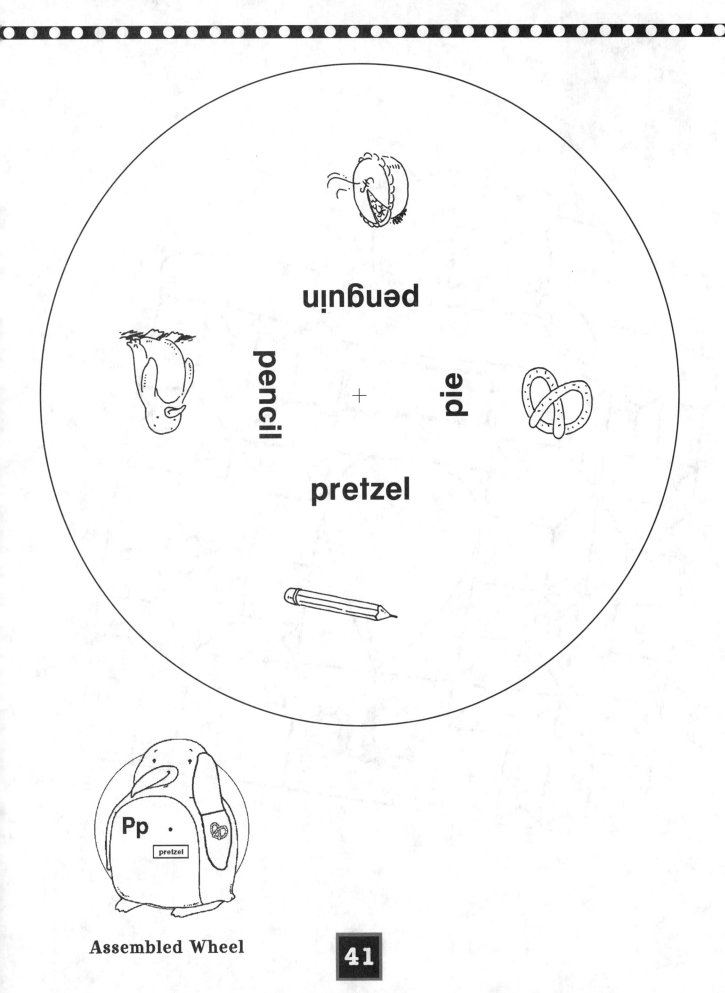

penguin

pencil

$+$

pie

pretzel

Pp

pretzel

Assembled Wheel

41

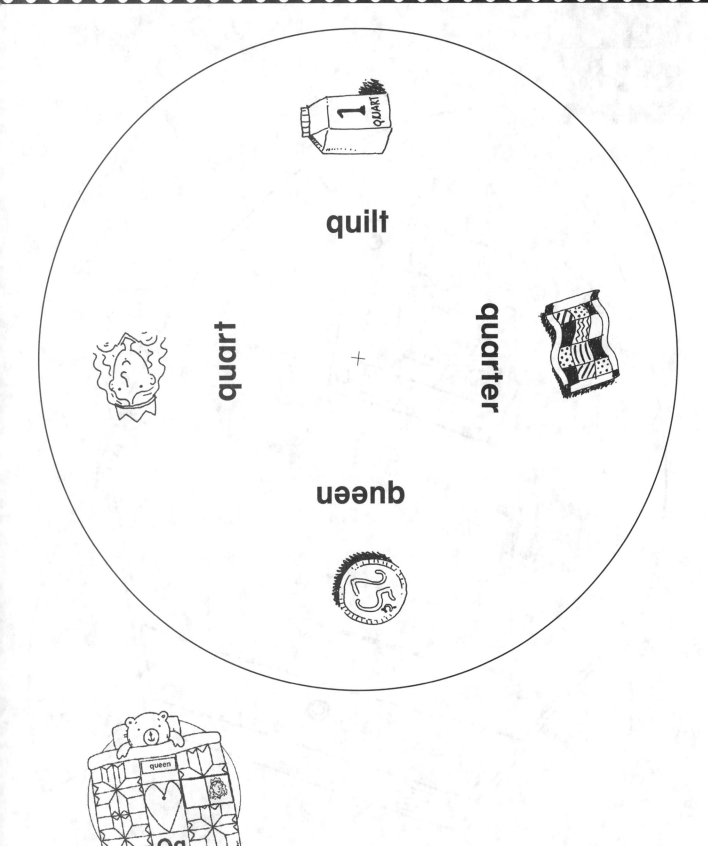

quilt

quart

quarter

queen

Assembled Wheel

43

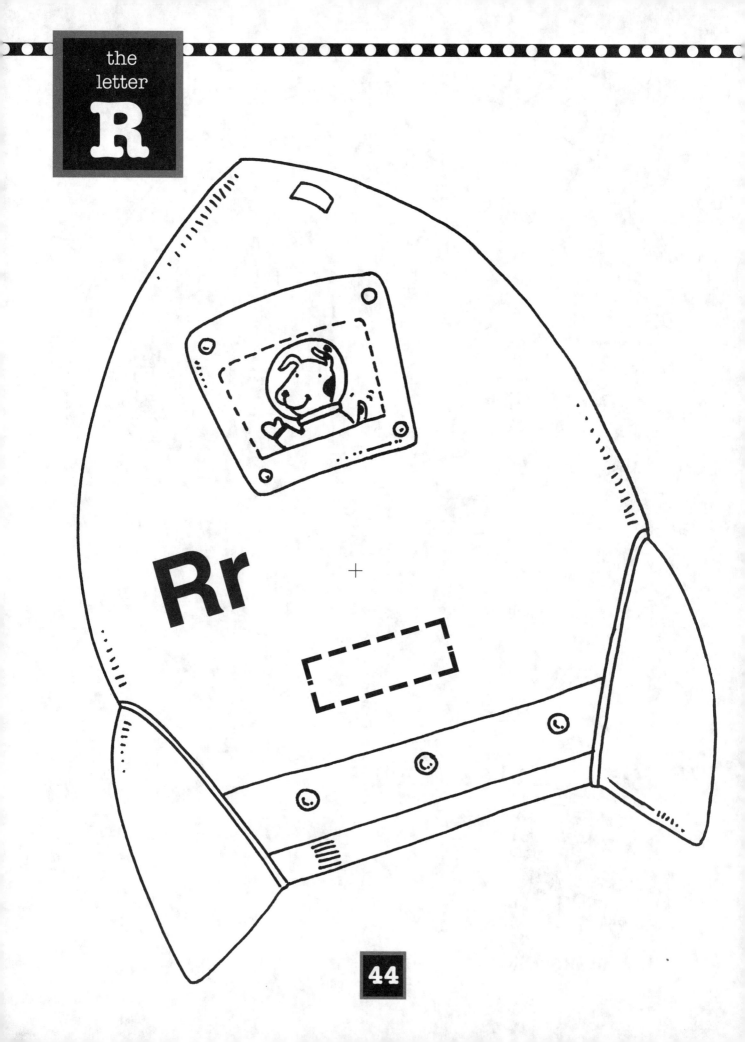

Rr

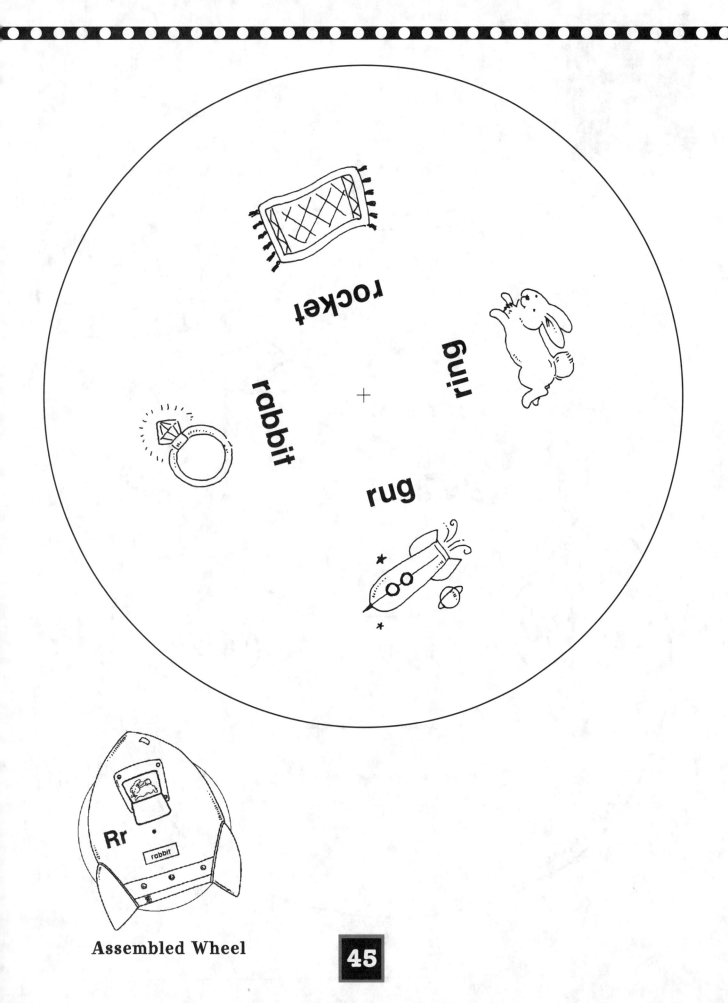

rocket

rabbit

ring

rug

Rr

rabbit

Assembled Wheel

45

Ss

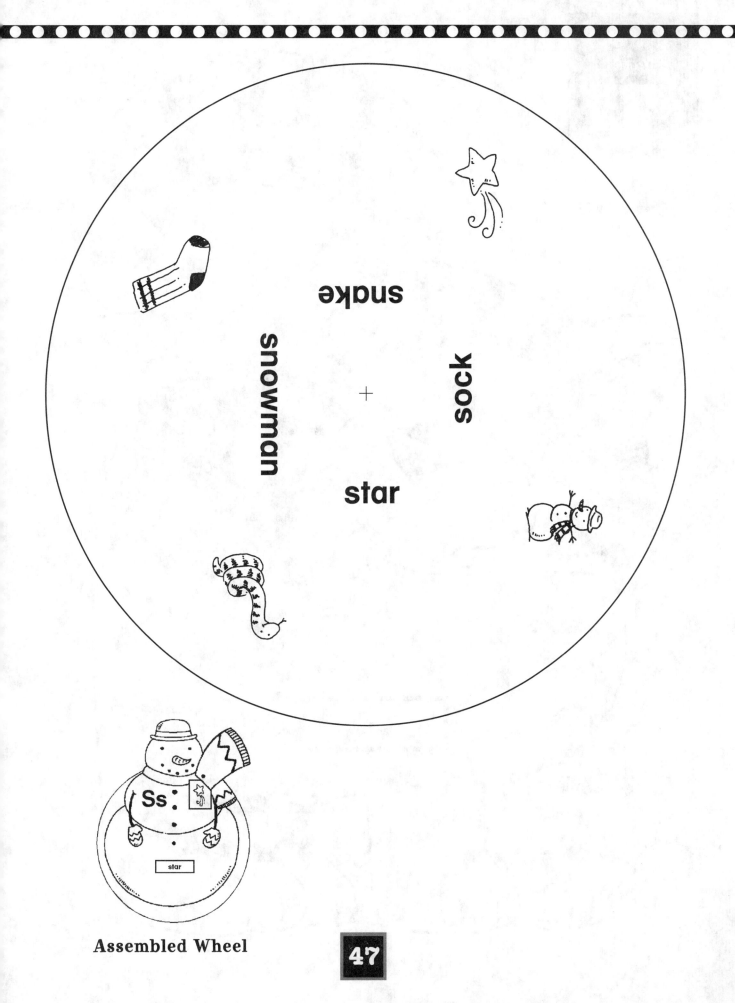

snake

sock

snowman

+

star

Ss

star

Assembled Wheel

Tt

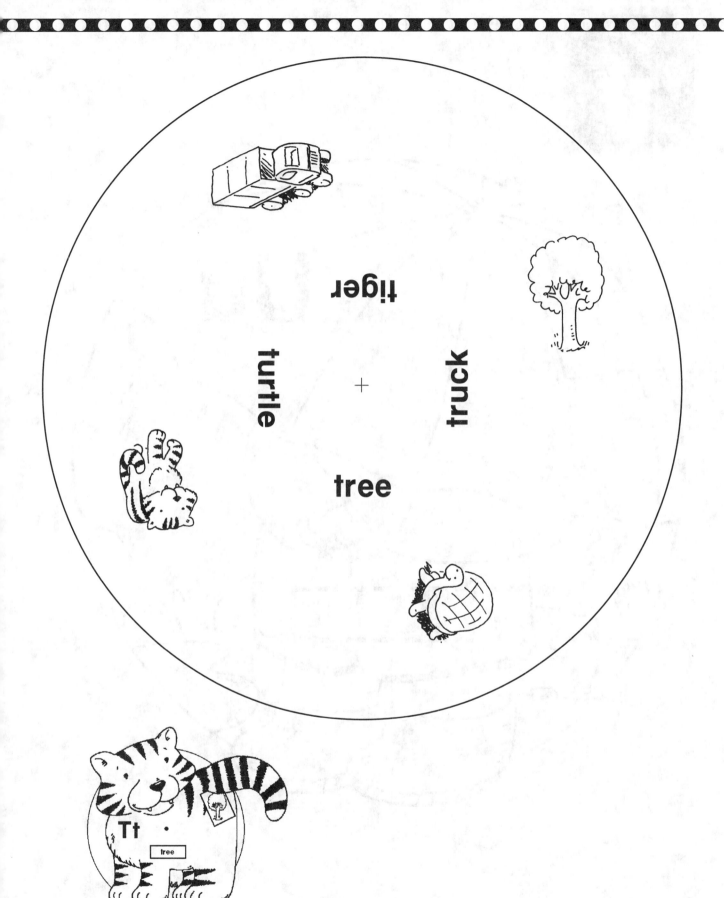

tiger

turtle ✛ truck

tree

Assembled Wheel

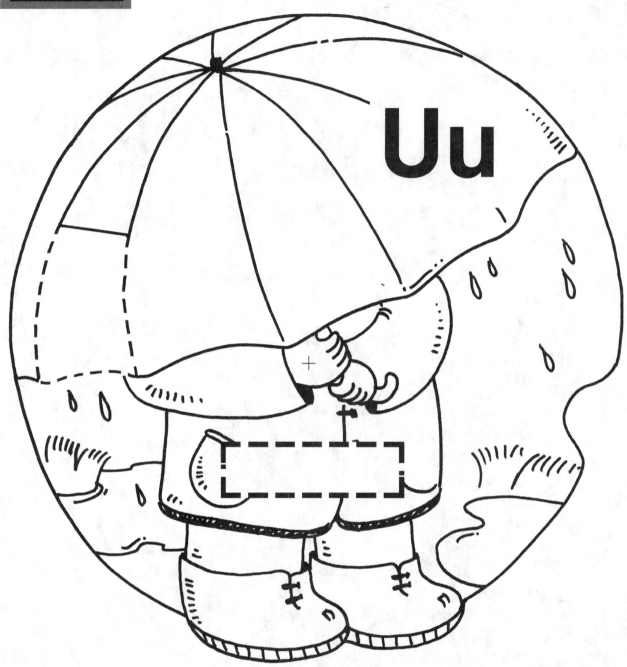

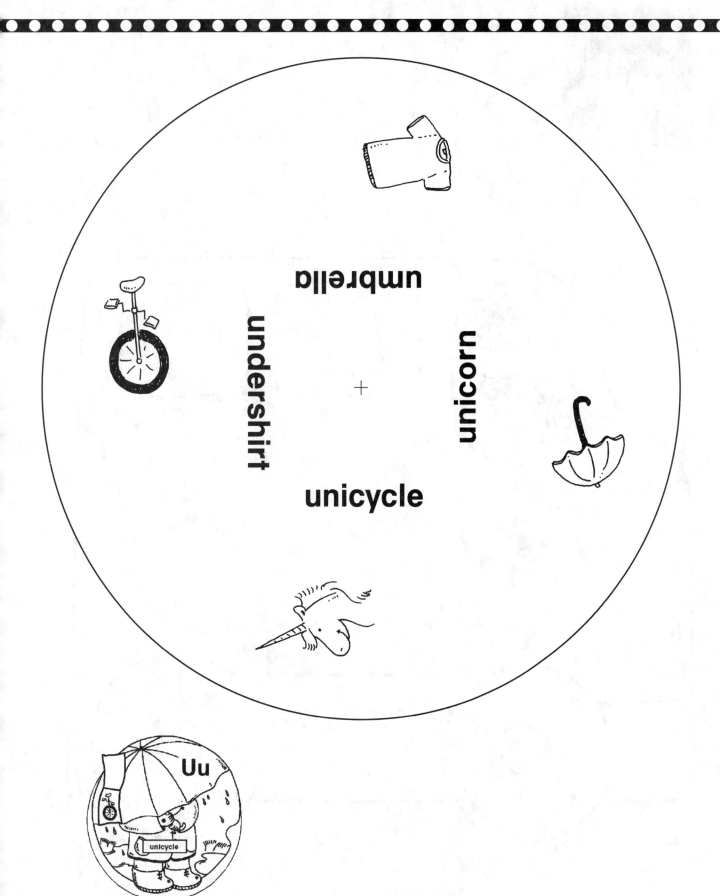

umbrella

undershirt

unicorn

+

unicycle

Uu

unicycle

Assembled Wheel

Vv

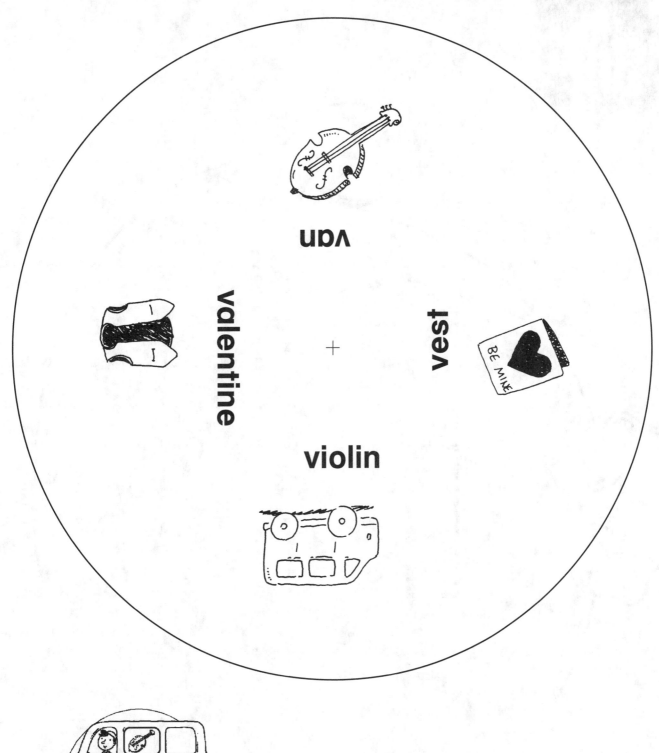

van

valentine

+

vest

violin

Assembled Wheel

53

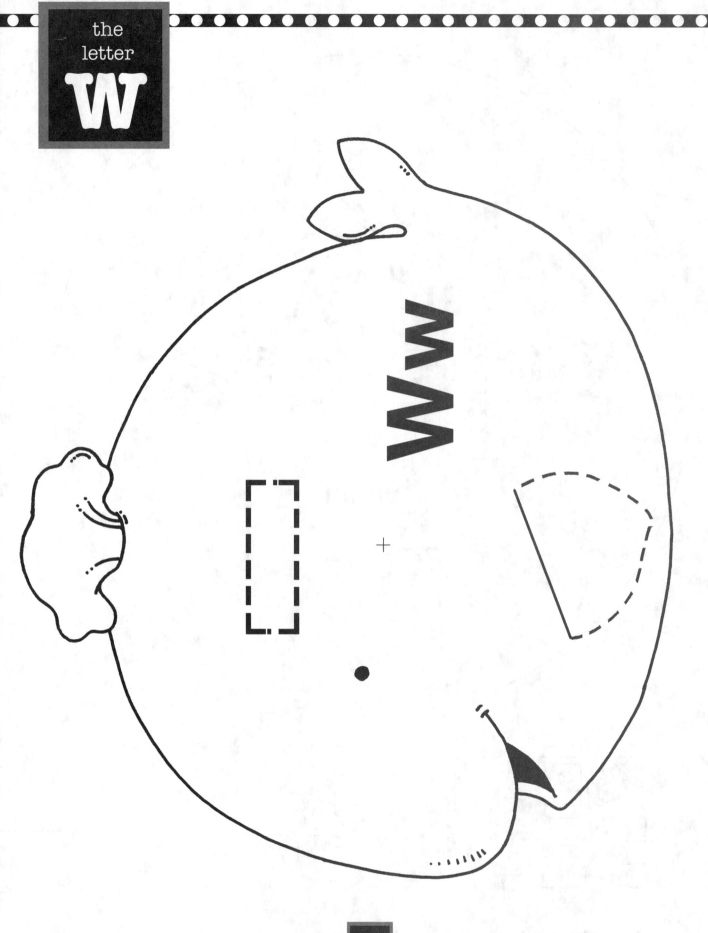

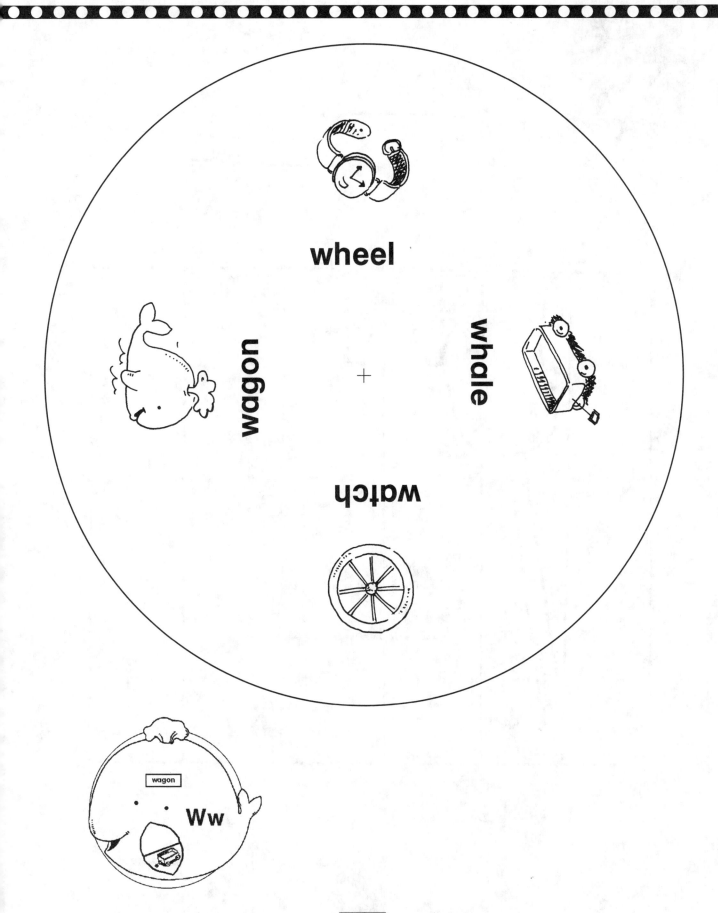

wheel

wagon

whale

watch

Assembled Wheel

55

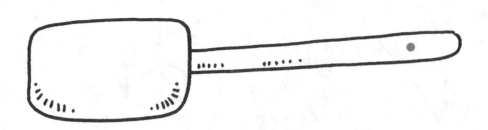

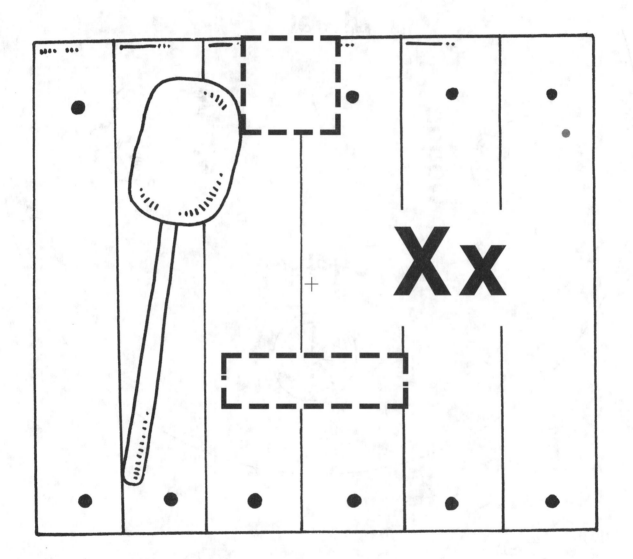

Xx

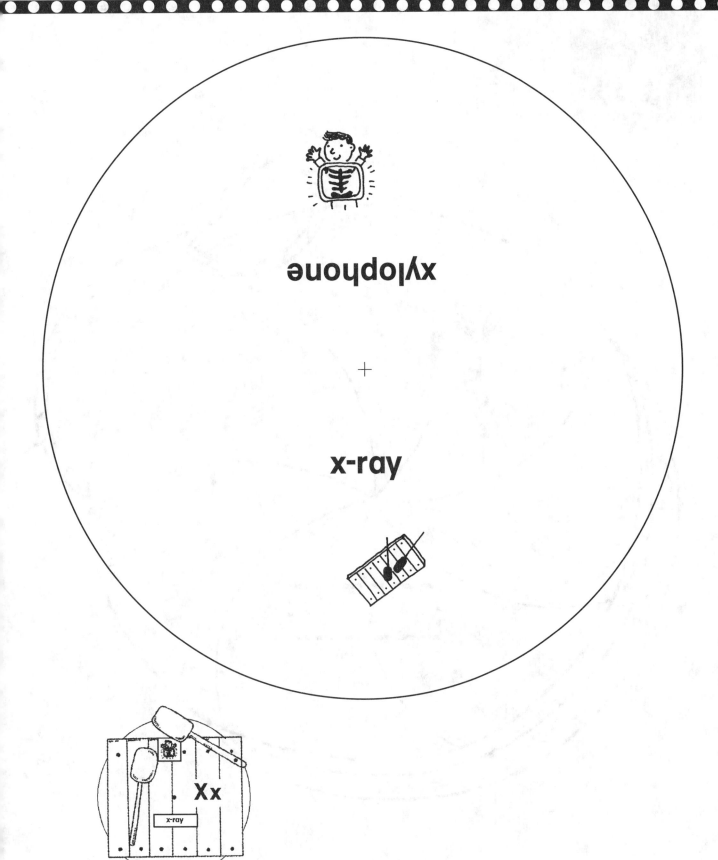

xylophone

+

x-ray

Xx

x-ray

Assembled Wheel

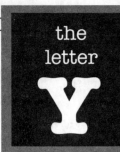

the
letter
Y

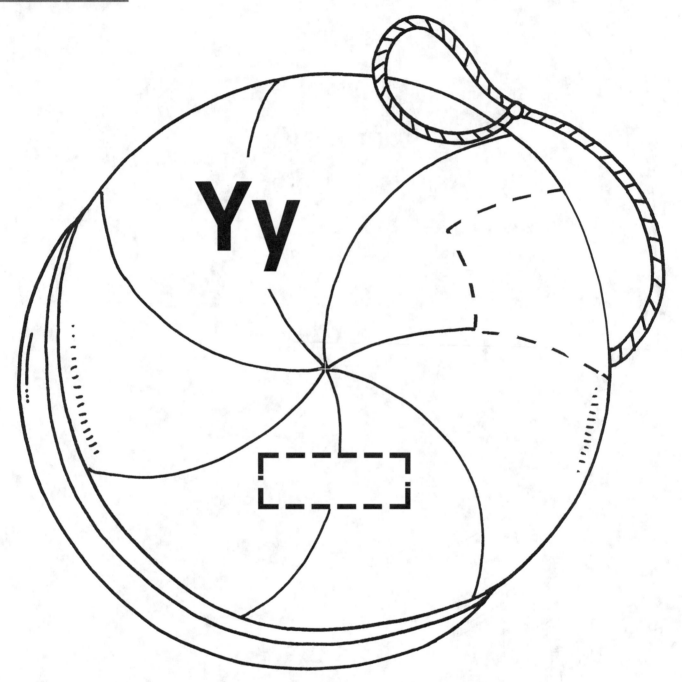

Yy

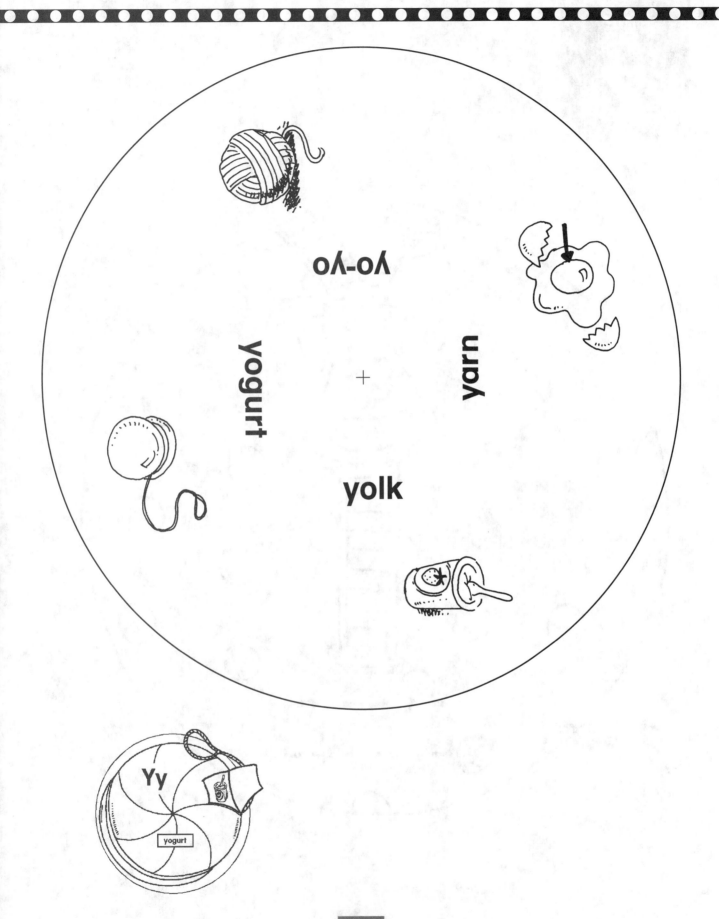

yo-yo

yarn

yogurt

+

yolk

Assembled Wheel

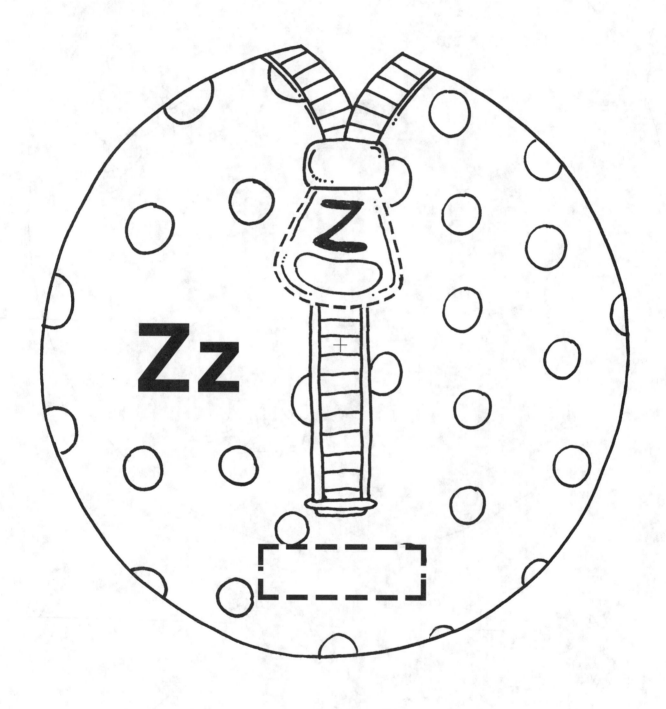

Zz

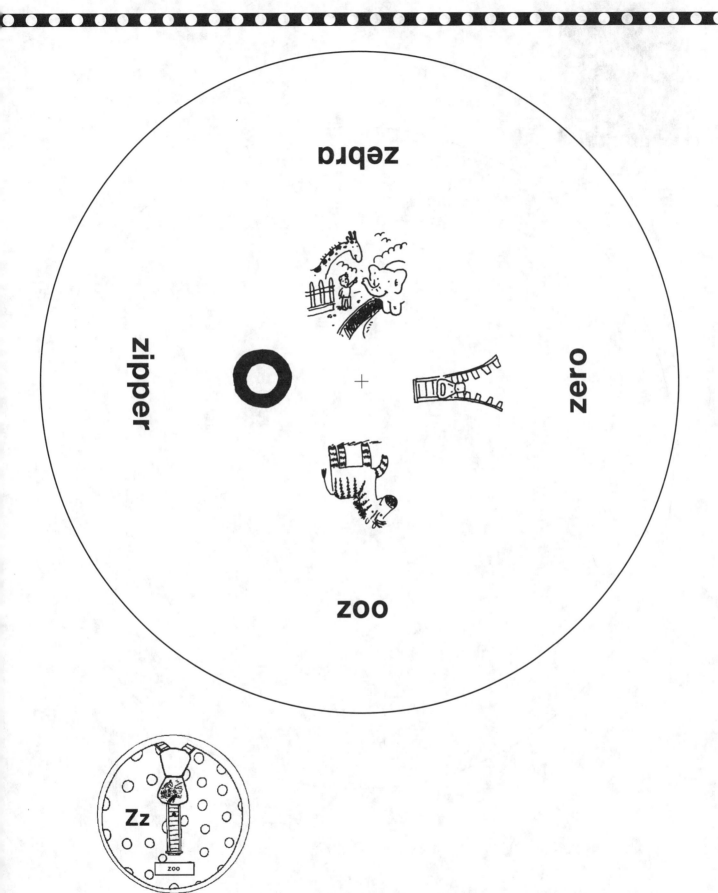

zebra

zipper

zero

zoo

Zz

zoo

Assembled Wheel

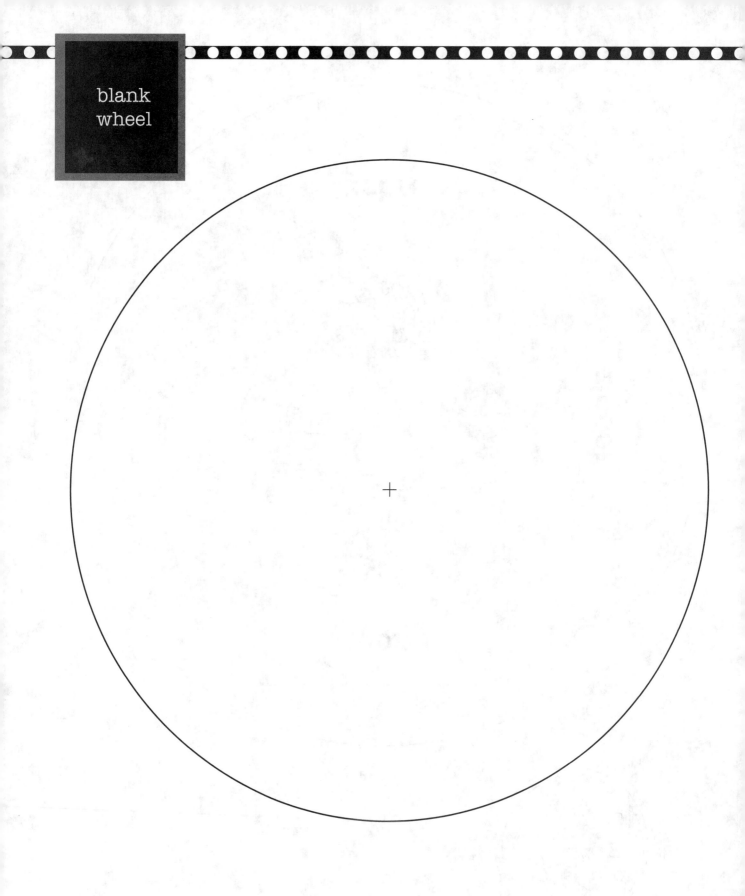